THE OFFICIAL CAT I.Q. TEST

THE OFFICIAL
CAT
I.Q. TEST

Peter Mandel

Illustrations by June Otani

HarperPerennial

A Division of HarperCollins*Publishers*

FIRST EDITION

Designed by Helene Berinsky

Library of Congress Cataloging-in-Publication Data
Mandel, Peter, 1957–
    The official cat IQ test / by Peter Mandel.–1st HarperPerennial ed.
        p. cm.
    ISBN 0-06-096592-4 (paper)
    1. Cats–Humor. 2. Intelligence tests–Humor. 3. Animal intelligence–
Humor. I. Title.
PN6231.C23M36 1991
818'.5407–dc20   90-55581

91 92 93 94 95 AM 10 9 8 7 6 5 4 3 2 1

For Kathy

Acknowledgments

The Official Cat I.Q. Test came about in large part through the assistance and support of my wife, Kathy. I'm also grateful to my brother, Geoff, and sister, Jenny, and to my two grandmothers, Rose Mandel and Liz Emslie.

Many of my friends provided much-needed inspiration, notably, Missy and John Berg, Pat and Ken Harrison, George Varga, and Marian Taylor.

Many thanks to my agent, Emilie Jacobson, and my editors, Larry Ashmead and Eamon Dolan, for believing in this bizarre project. Finally, I'd like to thank the following for their contributions to individual cat I.Q. questions: Rita Mae Brown, Ann Combs, Kevin Currie, Leonore Fleischer, Bette Harrison, Patrick Lewis, Craig Nelson, Ellen Sargent, and Vinnie Williams.

THE OFFICIAL CAT I.Q. TEST

Introduction

Those of us who live with cats have a hard time avoiding comparisons. "Mittens," we have been heard to say, "is the only cat in recorded history who knows how to use a trampoline. But he never figured out the sound of the electric can opener. Belle, on the other hand, starts meowing the instant I lift a can of chunk light tuna from the kitchen shelf . . ."

Some may see the need of scientific standards for comparing one animal to the next: today's cats with yesterday's, longhairs with shorthairs, Maine Coons with Siamese, the cat you have now with the cat you had in college, cats with dogs, cats with small children, and so on. I hope those who recognize this need will ignore *The Official Cat I.Q. Test*, for instead of turning up reliable data on feline intelligence, it will probably only provide you and your cat with a few well-earned laughs. If, however, the two of you have agreed not to take each other too seriously (and this is a good first step), why not cooperate further and give this easy and fun test a try?

In the end, I hope you will discover that your cat's I.Q. score—just like its meowings, yawnings, stretchings, scratchings, and comings and goings—reflects its unique personality.

If not, you have my permission to take the test over until you get it right.

—P.M.

Directions

Taking *The Official Cat I.Q. Test* should be a relatively painless experience for you and your cat. Respond to the following questions, awarding your pet 1 point for each "a" answer, 2 points for each "b" answer, 3 points for each "c" answer, and 4 points for each "d" answer. Then total up your cat's score and refer to the following highly scientific scale. Best of luck!

Rating Scale	Total I.Q. Score	Typical Characteristic
Genius	198-220	Solves ethical dilemmas
Intelligent	175-197	Forges lottery tickets
Above Average	151-174	Outsmarts most preteens
Average	127-150	Comes when called
Below Average	103-126	Still learning its name
Moderately Retarded	79-102	Walks into walls
Severely Retarded	55-78	Forgets how to meow

1. Place your cat in front of a mirror. It proceeds to:

 a) peer up, down—everywhere but at the mirror

 b) look behind the mirror for another cat

 c) show interest in its reflection

 d) do some primping and preening

2. Get down on all fours, bark loudly, and bare your teeth. Your cat:

 a) scrambles frantically to the top of the nearest chair

 b) fluffs up to look larger

 c) looks quizzically at you

 d) yawns

3. When you're preparing to use the vacuum cleaner, your cat:

    a) is underfoot

    b) is under stress

    c) is under the bed

    d) convinces you to use a sweeper instead

4. Place some Friskies under a paper cup and put down two more empty cups. Try to get your cat's attention as you mix up the cups. Your cat:

    a) ignores this little game

    b) knocks over the wrong cup

    c) knocks over the right cup

    d) makes you feel guilty and foolish for
       wasting its food

5. **When your cat relieves itself, it:**

    a) does so indiscriminately

    b) uses several depositories

    c) uses a single depository or box

    d) uses and flushes the toilet

6. **Your cat prefers to eat:**

    a) any slop

    b) its own food

    c) its own game

    d) contraband from the cupboard or
       refrigerator

7. **Put on a record or a CD. Your cat:**

    a) acts acutely deaf

    b) flattens its ears

    c) swishes its tail

    d) shakes its booty

8. Your cat usually does the following while you're watching "Wheel of Fortune":

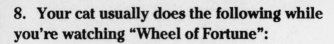

   a) meows at random

   b) meows at cat food commercials

   c) meows at Vanna White

   d) changes the channel

9. Your cat's favorite hiding place is:

a) in an open box

b) under the kitchen table

c) in the medicine cabinet

d) you've never found its favorite place

10. In order to wake you up, your cat:

a) meows quietly

b) knocks things over

c) sits on your head or chest

d) starts coffee brewing

11. A new Doberman pinscher has just moved in next door. Your cat:

a) saunters over to the dog's food bowl for some free munchies

b) meows menacingly

c) bares its teeth, arches its back, and, in general, makes itself look like The Cat From Hell

d) devises a clever—and ultimately fatal— booby trap for the hapless dog

12. Your cat's favorite pastime is playing with:

a) a scrap of paper

b) a piece of string

c) a ball of string

d) the home version of "Jeopardy!"

13. Your cat spies a cockroach crawling out of your cookie jar with a satisfied expression on its face. It proceeds to:

a) blink absentmindedly

b) smack its lips

c) pounce on the insect, leaving the cookies undisturbed

d) pounce on a cookie, leaving the insect

14. In the presence of someone acutely allergic and/or deathly afraid of cats, your cat:

    a) leaves the room

    b) crawls under the couch and stays there until the visitor has gone

    c) sits in the middle of the kitchen floor and stares at the intruder

    d) heads straight for its victim and showers him with lavish attention

15. On a frigid winter evening your cat:

    a) begs to go outdoors

    b) inhabits a drafty windowsill

    c) sneaks into the dryer you left open

    d) stretches out to completely cover the only heat register in the room

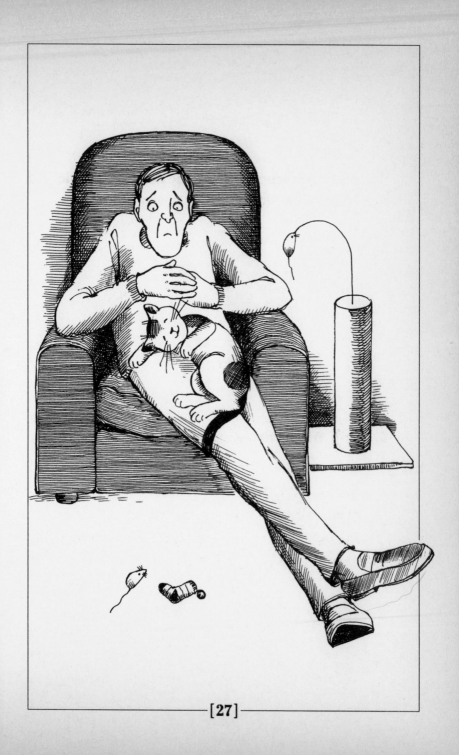

16. When a favorite person leaves home, your cat:

  a) seems not to notice his or her absence

  b) acts upset for a few days and then adjusts to the situation

  c) spends most of its time sleeping on the person's bed

  d) follows you around the house meowing, letting you know it holds you primarily responsible for driving the person away

17. Faced with an active two-year-old, your cat:

  a) submits to a death grip and allows itself to be lugged endlessly around the house

  b) lets the child pet it, but only gently

  c) insists that the child admire it from a distance of at least six feet

  d) checks into a motel until the child is safely gone

18. The largest "kill" your cat has ever dragged home is:

a) a newt

b) a pair of chipmunks

c) a family of muskrats

d) a bull mastiff, along with its collar and a piece of a chain-link fence

19. You are reading a newspaper in your favorite chair. Does your cat tend to:

a) sit at your feet

b) sit in your lap

c) lounge across the page

d) perch delicately on the arm of the chair, dangling its tail across the very sentence you are reading

20. Take your cat for a drive downtown in the family car. It:

    a) urinates on the upholstery

    b) crawls into the glove compartment

    c) critiques your driving from the back seat

    d) yells obscenities at passing motorcyclists

21. You walk into an upstairs room and find your cat out on the very edge of the window ledge. Your heart stops just as your cat:

    a) jumps, trusting in its nine lives

    b) balances on two legs

    c) blinks at you indifferently

    d) daintily leaps to your neighbor's window ledge

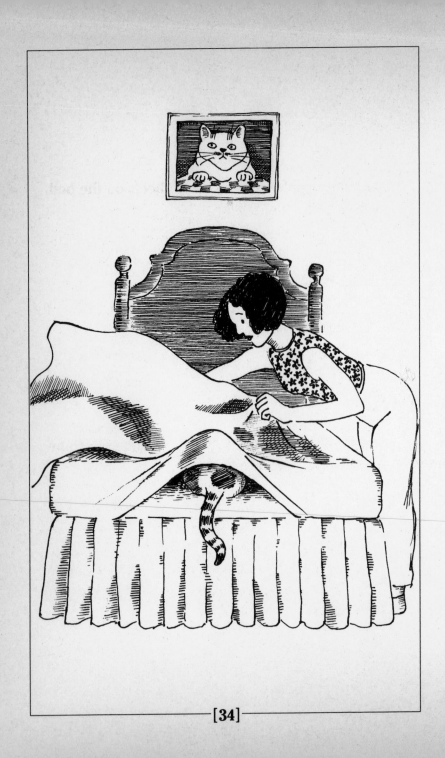

22. When you're putting clean sheets on the bed, your cat will most often:

   a) stare vacantly

   b) create an indoor blizzard of airborne cat hair

   c) jump up, slide under the bottom sheet, and force you to make the bed around it

   d) make secret plans to pee on the pillowcases

23. If you pet your cat when it doesn't wish to be petted, it responds by:

   a) glaring at you

   b) snapping at you

   c) neatly severing your jugular

   d) simply tolerating you and, when you stop, meticulously washing the contaminated spot

24. While bird-watching, your cat is most fascinated by:

    a) pigeons

    b) sparrows

    c) snowy egrets

    d) bald eagles

25. Held at arm's length, your cat most resembles:

    a) a bag of flour

    b) a feather pillow

    c) a trapeze artist

    d) a master of tae kwon do

26. Your veterinarian instructs you to give your cat a pill. The cat:

    a) laps it up

    b) chews it, then spits it out

    c) fights like a wounded tiger

    d) vanishes when you think "pill"

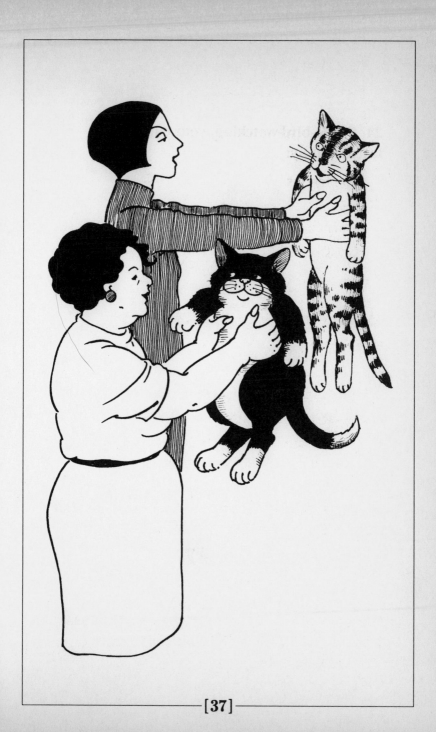

27. Next time your local store has a sale bring home two cases of your cat's favorite food. Your cat:

a) eats each and every can with gusto

b) eats its way enthusiastically through the first case but shows some reluctance with the second

c) refuses to touch a morsel of your supply

d) stops eating entirely—forcing you to purchase and prepare expensive treats, like Norwegian smoked salmon and fresh lobster bisque, in an attempt to revive its appetite

28. During stormy weather, open the front door to invite your cat to go out. It:

   a) scoots right out into the rain

   b) stands in the doorway for five minutes while monitoring the temperature, humidity, and wind velocity

   c) glances out briefly, then heads back to the sofa

   d) looks up moodily from its nap as if to say, "Are you insane?"

29. When confronted with a dripping faucet, your cat:

   a) thinks it's time for a shower

   b) studies each and every drip

   c) gingerly drinks from the tap without getting wet

   d) collects water in a glass for later

30. Your cat's favorite prey is:

a) wind-up mouse toys

b) open grocery bags

c) necklaces and bracelets

d) panty hose adorning the legs of house guests

31. When you return from vacation and your cat hasn't seen you for two weeks, it:

a) follows you everywhere, crying mournfully

b) follows you everywhere, complaining bitterly

c) follows you everywhere, scolding mercilessly

d) eats two bowls of food and sacks out

32. When in the hands of a veterinarian, which phrase best describes your cat's demeanor:

a) curious

b) curmudgeonly

c) cold and aloof

d) downright uncooperative

33. Your cat knows you prefer it to the family dog because:

   a) you tell it so, day in and day out

   b) it sleeps with you; the dog sleeps on the floor

   c) the dog never eats from your plate

   d) it's absolutely arrogant about these things

34. Your cat's favorite wintertime sport on TV seems to be:

   a) professional wrestling

   b) roller derby

   c) college basketball

   d) chess

35. Place a good-sized pinch of catnip next to your cat's food bowl. Your cat:

    a) sneezes violently

    b) samples a couple of mouthfuls

    c) takes a hearty whiff and rolls over

    d) becomes ecstatic and passes out for a
       day and a half

36. **Next time you're flipping through the FM radio dial, study your cat's reactions to the various station formats. Your cat seems to prefer:**

   a) easy listening with Larry Loungelizard

   b) country/western with Skitch McBracken

   c) top 40 with Play-it-Again Sam

   d) chamber music with C.D. Aficionado

37. **When the doorbell rings, your cat:**

   a) races to answer the phone

   b) salivates

   c) hides in the coat closet

   d) stretches up to the keyhole and does a
      pretty fair imitation of a snarling Doberman

38. **The feline your cat most admires is:**

   a) Jane Pauley's cat Meatball

   b) Gerald Ford's cat Shan

   c) Winston Churchill's cat Jock

   d) Albert Einstein's cat Sizi

39. When the telephone rings, your cat:

   a) runs to answer the door

   b) salivates

   c) carefully carries the instrument to the nearest family member

   d) lifts the receiver and cracks, "Tony's pizza. Can I take your order?"

40. Pull out your cat's brush or comb and begin a grooming session. Your cat:

   a) begins purring because it loves the attention

   b) begins growling because you're tugging at knots and tangles

   c) begins hissing because this isn't the time it had scheduled for grooming

   d) provides detailed styling instructions

41. When you bring home a new date, your cat:

a) makes friends immediately

b) shows off slightly by rolling onto its back

c) launches into a frenzy of acrobatics

d) expresses disdain by painstakingly cleaning its anus

42. Next time you host the neighborhood poker game, cut the deck and deal your cat a hand. It:

a) seems more interested in the box the cards came in

b) uses its paw to do some shuffling

c) passes you back two cards, suggesting it has three of a kind

d) produces five aces

43. A day at the beach for your cat is a day spent:

    a) paddling around in the undertow

    b) hiding under a beach blanket

    c) digging moon-sized craters

    d) looking for 98-pound weaklings to kick sand at

44. Offered a choice of leftovers from several restaurants (we try to avoid using the term "doggie bag"), your cat selects:

    a) Luke's Luau Hut

    b) Bob's Big Boy

    c) Trader Vic's

    d) Lutèce

45. Present your thirsty cat with water in four different receptacles. It prefers to drink from:

a) the bowl

b) the mug that says, "Have a Nice Day!"

c) the pan that you boil water for coffee in

d) the Wedgwood goblet you got as a
   wedding present

46. When the family gathers for a quiet evening around the crackling hearth, your cat's favorite activity seems to be:

a) swallowing marbles

b) swatting checkers

c) agitating knitting needles

d) creating origami sculpture

47. Bring out your ironing board and a hot iron. Your cat:

  a) stretches across the board, ready to be ironed

  b) asks to be misted

  c) dives into the laundry basket

  d) hides the spray starch

48. If you had to recognize one subject as your cat's field of expertise, it would probably be:

  a) entomology

  b) ornithology

  c) marine biology

  d) Egyptology

49. If your cat could take up a human hobby it would be most likely to choose:

    a) rock polishing

    b) beer brewing

    c) butterfly collecting

    d) bonsai cultivation

50. Which popular mail-order catalog does your cat prefer to find shredded in its litterbox (judging by volume of production):

    a) Sears

    b) Lillian Vernon

    c) F.A.O. Schwarz

    d) Hammacher Schlemmer

51. When your cat spends the night in a hotel or motel, it tends to:

    a) hang out at the ice machine

    b) lounge by the pool

    c) ask for quarters to use "Magic Fingers"

    d) phone in bogus wake-up calls

52. During the summer months, your cat prefers to tune in to:

    a) stock car racing

    b) celebrity golf

    c) water polo

    d) cricket

53. Tranquilized and put on a plane, your cat usually winds up:

    a) diverted, by mistake, to LaGuardia

    b) sharing the baggage compartment with a German shepherd

    c) making mournful noises under your seat

    d) drinking Scotch in the cockpit with the flight engineer

54. Your cat shows you the greatest affection:

a) when you call it saying, "Here, kitty, kitty"

b) in the evening, when you're sitting in your favorite chair

c) at mealtime

d) when you're dressed head to toe in something newly cleaned and either navy blue or black

55. If you bring a new cat into your household, your cat will most likely:

a) make friends with it

b) shy away from it

c) shy away from you

d) go into long-term therapy